Olympics 2002

Other Books in the Sports Heroes Series

Olympics 2002

Mark Littleton

Zonderkidz

Zonder**kidz**™

The children's group of Zondervan

www.zonderkidz.com

Sports Heroes: Olympics 2002
Copyright © 2002 by Mark Littleton

Requests for information should be addressed to:
Grand Rapids, Michigan 49530

ISBN: 0–310–70294–1

Editor: Barbara Scott
Art direction: Lisa Workman
Cover design: Alan Close
Cover photography: Mike Powell / Allsport
Interior design: Todd Sprague
Interior photography: Allsport

Printed in the United States of America

02 03 04 05 06 07 /❖DC/ 10 9 8 7 6 5 4 3 2 1

ACKNOWLEDGMENTS

Thanks to Robyne Baker for helping me round up these interviews. Thanks to my wife for her insights on editing. Thanks to my kids for not tempting me too much to play Rummikub when I had to be writing.

To Thurman Jr., Vangie, Amelia,
and Lydia Gardner.
You make all of us so happy. Thanks.

CONTENTS

PARIS - LYON - MEDITERRANEE

Auguste Matisse

AUX VAINQUEURS DU CONCOURS DE LA VIIIme OLYMPIADE
CHAMONIX-MONT-BLANC
25 Janvier-5 Février 1924

1

THE FIRST OLYMPICS

Have you ever wondered about the historical origin of the sports spectacular we call the Olympics?

The first Olympics were held in 776 B.C. near Olympia, Greece, and consisted of just one 200-yard footrace. At that time, only Greek citizens were allowed to participate. Winners received laurel wreaths for first (today's gold medal), a wild olive wreath for second (today's silver), and a palm wreath for third (today's bronze). It was the first year the Greeks began keeping a calendar of Olympiads or groups of four years. The Romans continued the tradition, but their methods deteriorated into virtual carnivals that bore little resemblance to the original pattern. In A.D. 394, Emperor Theodosius banned the games as disgusting celebrations not fit for Roman tradition.

The first modern Olympics were held in Athens in 1896. Baron Pierre de Coubertin, who initiated the games and designed the flag, wanted to promote culture and education while encouraging international relations. Thirteen nations competed in the first summer Olympics. The first winter Olympics opened on January 25, 1924, in Chamonix, France. Two hundred and ninety-four athletes (just eleven of them women) from sixteen countries competed. Although there were fourteen events, women were allowed to compete in only two of them: singles and pairs figure skating.

Olympic Symbols

The Olympics are rich with symbols, including the following:

- *The five Olympic rings* symbolize the five major continents—Europe, Asia, Africa, Australia, and America. Each ring is a different color—yellow, green, black, blue, and red.
- *The Olympic flag* consists of the five rings on a white background.
- *The Olympic motto* is "Citius, Altius, Fortius," which is a Latin phrase meaning "Swifter, Higher, Stronger."

- *The Olympic creed* states, "The most important thing in the Olympic Games is not to win but to take part, just as the most important thing in life is not the triumph but the struggle. The essential thing is not to have conquered but to have fought well."
- *The Olympic oath* states, "In the name of all competitors, I promise that we will take part in these Olympic Games, respecting and abiding by the rules that govern them, in the true spirit of sportsmanship for the glory of sport and the honor of our teams."
- *The Olympic flame* symbolizes the continuation of what started in Greece almost three millennia ago. The flame was first featured in 1936. The torch is lit by the sun's rays in Olympia, Greece, and then brought to the place of the Games by runners in successive relays through the cities of the world. To participate is a great honor. Ships and planes are used when required.

The Olympic Flag

The Olympic flag, consisting of five joined colored rings on a white background, was designed by Pierre de Coubertin, the initiator and founder of the modern Olympics. The six colors on the flag—blue, black, green, yellow, red, and white—were selected because one or more of these colors are used on every flag in the world. The symbol of the five rings joined together symbolizes the five continents in harmony with one another as athletes from around the world compete together as one unique whole. Amazingly, de Coubertin created this design without ever saying this was his plan.

The Winter Olympics

The Winter Olympics have been held in the following locations:

1924	Chamonix, France
1928	St. Moritz, Switzerland
1932	Lake Placid, New York
1936	Garmisch-Partenkirchen, Germany
1948	St. Moritz, Switzerland
1952	Oslo, Norway
1956	Cortina d'Ampezzo, Italy
1960	Squaw Valley, California
1964	Innsbruck, Austria
1968	Grenoble, France
1972	Sapporo, Japan
1976	Innsbruck, Austria
1980	Lake Placid, New York
1984	Sarajevo, Yugoslavia
1988	Calgary, Alberta, Canada
1992	Albertville, France
1994	Lillehammer, Norway
1998	Nagano, Japan
2002	Salt Lake City, Utah

For more information about the events, venues, and athletes at the 2002 Olympic Winter Games in Salt Lake City, Utah, check out the official website at www.SaltLake2002.com.

Final Medal Standings
1998 Olympics in Nagano, Japan

National Standing

Nation	Gold	Silver	Bronze	Total
Germany	12	9	8	29
Norway	10	10	5	25
Russia	9	6	3	18
Austria	3	5	9	17
Canada	6	5	4	15
U.S.A.	6	3	4	13
Finland	2	4	6	12
Netherlands	5	4	2	11
Japan	5	1	4	10
Italy	2	6	2	10
France	2	1	5	8
China	0	6	2	8
Switzerland	2	2	3	7
Others	5	6	11	22
Totals:	**69**	**68**	**68**	**205**

2

ALPINE SKIING

How did the sport of alpine skiing begin?
There is evidence that adventurers
strapped skis on their feet some five
thousand years ago, and many believe Norwe-
gians used skis to help them hunt in snowy ter-
rain. Skiing, primarily cross-country, spread to
Scandinavia and Russia as a means of trans-
portation and in time as a sport. Alpine skiing
developed as cross-country skiers learned to ski
faster and faster on downhill slopes. The first
competitions, which featured various types of
downhill courses, were featured in the 1850s in
Oslo, Norway. In the next thirty years, the sport
gained popularity throughout Europe and
became known in the United States, where min-
ers staged skiing competitions during the winter.

Englishman Sir Arnold Lunn and Austrian
Hannes Schneider were the creators of alpine
racing. Lunn, the son of a London travel agent,
often passed through the Alps on business and

began to think the range would make a perfect spot for skiing competitions. He called for all competitors to come to the first slalom in 1922 in Muerren, Switzerland. Two years later, he and Schneider organized the race that would become the first Olympic alpine event—the Arlberg-Kandahar, which combined slalom and downhill skiing.

World Championships for men's downhill and slalom events were first offered in 1931. Planners included women's alpine events for the first time in 1950. In 1966, Serge Lang, along with French ski coach Honore Bonnet and U.S. ski coach Bob Beattie, came together to plan the first FIS World Cup, which had its first competitive season in 1966–67.

Alpine skiing was added to the Olympic program at the 1936 Garmisch-Partenkirchen Games in Germany.

The first alpine skiing events in the Olympic program were a men's and women's combined competition, with both a downhill race and two slalom runs. After the 1940 and 1944 Olympic Games were canceled because of World War II, alpine skiing was revived at the St. Moritz Olympics in 1948, and five more events were added. The Oslo Games in 1952 brought in a giant slalom program that replaced the combined competition. In 1988, organizers decided to return the combined event to the program and then added the super-G to complete the ten-event competition present in today's Olympic Games.

Perhaps because of their location at the foot of the Alps, the nations of Western Europe have won the greatest number of Olympic medals in alpine skiing. Austria leads with seventy-seven, including twenty-four golds. Switzerland has earned forty-eight, and France has taken home thirty-seven.

The Main Events

There are five distinct competitions included in Olympic alpine racing:

Downhill—The downhill is the fastest of all alpine races; skiers attain speeds above one hundred miles per hour on downhill slopes.

How does it work? An International Ski Federation (FIS) official sets the course as he sees fit. In other races, a representative of one of the competing nations is responsible for this task. The gates in a downhill are marked by red flags, indicating where the skier must turn. (In other races, the flags alternate between blue and red.) There are no regulations concerning how far apart the flags should be.

To protect the skiers, the course is cleared of all obstacles, but frequently officials will strew pine needles along the course to help racers see further ahead. This tactic is helpful when a downhill skier goes airborne and is trying to land. The sides of the course may also be networked with padding and netting to cushion a fall and prevent a racer from slipping into the trees.

Prior to race day, for safety purposes, downhill skiers are allowed to run two practice races on the course. No other race allows practice runs. On race day, competitors may get a feel for the slope by "walking" through the course on their skis.

Super-G—The super-G (super-giant slalom) is the second fastest of all alpine races and features longer distances between gates than a giant slalom. The course must have at least thirty-five changes of direction for the men and a minimum of thirty changes of direction for the women. Alternating red and blue flags mark the gates of the super-G.

The course-setter is chosen from among the competing nations by way of a draw. After the last super-G competition prior to the Games, a drawing takes place to determine the nationality of the course-setter. The country of each super-G racer ranked in the top fifteen (determined by the World Cup start list) is put down on paper. The slip drawn determines the nationality of the course-setter.

Skiers are allowed to inspect the course on race day, but there are no practice runs. Athletes must memorize the course, find the fastest line (the path a skier takes through a course), and simply trust their discipline and instincts to get them through.

Giant Slalom—The giant slalom is the third fastest of the alpine races, requiring greater skill in edging and fast turning. Two giant slalom courses are set by two individuals from different countries. The nationalities are chosen by random drawing, as with the super-G. In the giant slalom, the vertical drop of the course determines how many turns will be placed on the course. Officials figure the vertical drop or altitude change by subtracting the elevation at the finish from the elevation at the starting gate. The courses are normally set the day before the race.

Slalom—The slalom is the most challenging alpine race in terms of dexterity, speed, and ability to turn sharp corners. Two slalom courses are set in the same way as the giant slalom with representatives from different nations leading.

From fifty-five to seventy-five gates dot the course in a men's race, while a women's course calls for forty-five to sixty-five gates. The courses are normally set the day before the race.

Combined—The combined competition brings together the slalom with all its turns and the downhill, which has none. The same rules govern how the courses are set.

The Olympic downhill trail features both courses, with different starting points. The men's combined downhill course starts at the women's downhill start house. The women's combined starts at a point below the men's. Both courses come together at the same finish line. In the same way, the slalom races within the combined event are set up on the downhill trail, with the women starting below the men.

Downhill
Super Giant Slalom
Giant Slalom
Slalom
Combined

Great Alpine Skiers

There are a number of skiers who have achieved greatness in Olympic competitions.

Penny Pitou

Penelope "Penny" Pitou started skiing at the age of five. Soon she was zipping down mountains on barrel staves cinched together with rubber bands. She loved to ski and longed to make the U.S. Olympic Ski Team and compete in the 1956 Winter Olympics.

Penny worked out like a woman on a mission, filling her days with bicycling, running, and mountain climbing. Her hard work paid off when she won a place on the 1956 Olympic team. She didn't earn a medal that year, but used the experience to prepare for the 1960 Olympics in Squaw Valley, California.

Training under coach David Lawrence in Aspen, Colorado, Penny got herself in the greatest shape of her life. She felt ready and primed for success.

The downhill that year featured a course that dropped 1,814 feet, and then planed out into a mile run. Three-quarters of the way into the course stood a perilous ninety-degree angle called "Airplane Corner." Right before Penny was scheduled to ski, she learned that fourteen previous skiers had wiped out on Airplane Corner. She was determined not to let it happen to her.

As Penny bolted downward in a screen of powder, that ninety-degree turn loomed big in her mind. When she reached it, though, she was ready. She held the course and completed the downhill in a good time of 1:38:6. Only Heidi Beibl of Germany ranked higher, and Penny won the silver.

Over all the runs that year, Penny clocked well and took a silver in the giant slalom. Her friend Betsy Snite beat the field in the slalom. That year,

FEBRUARY
21
1980

On This Day In Olympic History

The little country of Liechtenstein won its first gold medal in Olympic history. Hanni Wenzel took first in the giant slalom.

the U.S. Women's Ski Team took more medals than any other competing country.

Penny had come a long way from barrel staves. The countless hours of conditioning and plunging down mountains at breakneck speeds had paid off—both for Penny and for the United States.

Jean-Claude Killy

Named to the French Legion of Honor, Jean-Claude Killy was a dashing, robust hero, known the world over. His nickname, "Casse-cou" (*Breakneck* in French), characterized everything he did in life. Today, he presides over a business empire worth close to a billion dollars.

But 1968 was the year that clinched his fame. What happened?

Killy grew up in the village of Val d'Isere at his father's ski lodge, and was skiing by the age of three. Nothing made him happier than whooshing down the side of a mountain at top speed, leaving the competition in a cloud of snow. At age fifteen, he dropped out of school to ski full time.

The 1968 Winter Olympic Games were held in the French Alps at Grenoble. Killy had already won twenty-three of thirty major races in the 1966–67 season. He was considered to be an overwhelming favorite for the gold medal, even though in the 1964 Innsbruck Winter Olympic Games, he completed only one race, taking fifth place in the giant slalom.

While serving in the French Army in Algeria in 1962, Killy had contracted hepatitis and amebic dysentery. His condition had badly hampered his performance in 1964. But by 1968, he was healthy and skiing at the top of his game.

Killy's potential was widely discussed. Would he win the gold? Would he win two golds? Three? Only one other skier had garnered three medals—Austrian Toni Sailer in the 1956 Olympics in Cortina d'Ampezzo, Italy. Two major contenders stood in Killy's way. Guy Perillat excelled in the downhill, and Karl Schranz of Germany dominated the slalom. Nearly everyone thought Killy would take the giant slalom.

FEBRUARY
25
1980

On This Day In Olympic History

Italian slalom racer Alberto Tomba took golds in the slalom and giant slalom at the Olympics in Calgary, Alberta, Canada. His finish of .06 seconds faster than anyone else in the slalom was the smallest margin of victory ever in a men's alpine event.

men's combined and a silver in the slalom. But 1984 was to be his year.

Phil and Steve grew up in White Pass, Washington, and began skiing at an early age. In 1973, at the age of fifteen, Phil became a member of the U.S. Ski Team. Disaster struck, though, when he was caught in an avalanche and broke his leg. He missed the 1974 season. In 1975, Phil broke the same leg again in a fall and missed most of the 1975 season. Finally, late in 1975, he won the U.S. National Giant Slalom title.

In 1976 he traveled to Innsbruck for the 1976 Olympic Games, where he placed fifth in the giant slalom. He was just eighteen years old. More disasters struck in 1979. Phil broke his left ankle in a Lake Placid competition. Doctors used seven screws and a two-inch plate to hold it together.

A year later, Phil won the gold in the alpine combined and silver in slalom at the Olympic Games in Lake Placid, New York. Over the next three years (1981-83), Phil won three consecutive overall World Cup titles.

The Olympic Games in Sarajevo looked promising for Phil. He announced he would retire after the upcoming Games, but he was primed for competition.

One hundred and one skiers prepared for the final event: the slalom. Heavy snowfall created a maze in the course, making it treacherous. Many

Killy wowed them all. The downhill was first. Perillat led, with an excellent time, but Killy, pushing hard, won with .08 seconds to spare.

Three days later, Killy took the giant slalom with aplomb, earning his nickname "Breakneck" once again as he careened down the mountain.

The last event, the slalom, was shrouded in a thick fog on the day of the race. The sun broke through only momentarily as Killy posted the best time in the first run. Hakon Mjoen of Norway, however, bested Killy's time and was about to take the gold when the cameras revealed he had missed two gates. He was disqualified.

Next, Austrian Karl Schranz, the favorite, also looked good until an unauthorized person appeared on the course in front of him. He had to make a rerun. This he did, beating Killy. However, the judges noticed that Schranz had also missed two gates before stopping on his first run. He was disqualified and Killy took all three gold medals—downhill, slalom, and giant slalom. Some say he was and is the greatest skier of all time.

Phil Mahre

Phil and Steve Mahre, twin brothers born four minutes apart, dominated the international world of skiing in the late 1970s and early 1980s. In the 1980 Olympics, Phil Mahre took a gold in the skiers wiped out during the competition. Steve led with a time of 50.85. Phil trailed with a 51.55 (third place behind Sweden's Jonas Nilsson).

Then, on his second run, Phil skied brilliantly and slid into first place. Only his brother, Steve, could do better. At the bottom, Phil communicated with Steve by walkie-talkie, telling him how to win the race. Incredibly, one brother was telling the other brother how to win it all. It was the way they had always been.

Going for broke, Steve hurtled down the course. He did well but not well enough. He finished second overall after Phil, who won the gold.

A few minutes before he stood on the platform to receive the gold medal, friends informed Phil that his first son had just been born. It was an emotional moment, seeing the American flag raised, hearing the National Anthem being played, winning the gold medal, and becoming a father, but Phil and Steve stood strong and proud. The Mahre twins won gold and silver that day, the final volley of a great career for Phil.

Olympic Watch

Erik Schlopy

Pronunciation: SCHLO-pee
Birth date: August 21, 1972
Birthplace: Buffalo, New York

Country: United States
Residence: Park City, Utah
Height: 5'10" (178 cm)
Weight: 185 lbs. (84 kg)

Erik Schlopy was just nineteen years old when he won two national titles—giant slalom and super-G—in the same year, 1992. However, his performance two years later at the Lillehammer Games was disappointing. He fell on his first slalom run and placed thirty-fourth in giant slalom.

In 1995 Erik left the U.S. Olympic Team to see if he could make it in professional racing. "It wasn't any one particular thing, like a conflict with a coach or a specific situation that drove me to quit," he says. "I was unhappy with myself and didn't always know why. I just had a vision of not going anywhere and I didn't want that to happen." Erik competed professionally for the next three years, but when he learned that the 2002 Olympic Winter Games were to take place in Utah, his home state, he came back to the World Cup competition for the 1999–2000 season.

Erik quickly reclaimed Olympic eligibility and posted strong results. In the 1999–2000 season, he did well in the slalom, winning a national title, and making it into the top ten in World Cup competition. In 2000–2001 he posted his best World Cup results with a second-place finish in the giant slalom in Bormio, Italy, on December 21.

Sarah Schleper

Pronunciation: SHLEP-er
Birth date: February 19, 1979
Birthplace: Glenwood Springs, Colorado
Country: United States
Residence: Vail, Colorado
Height: 5'4" (163 cm)
Weight: 140 lbs. (64 kg)

Sarah was just two years old when she was given her first pair of skis. Raised by a single dad, a ski bum himself, she received plenty of encouragement to learn and excel in the sport. She began racing at age eleven, and made her World Cup debut at age sixteen.

Gaining a reputation as a top technical skier, Sarah placed second in the slalom at the Junior World Championships in 1997. Soon after, she raced in her first Olympic competition, the 1998 Nagano Games, and finished twenty-second in the same event.

A fall on the slopes in December of 1998 left Sarah with a compression fracture of her right tibia, a torn ligament, and a strained ligament in her right knee. She was unable to compete in the 1998–99 World Cup season. "The biggest shock was when the doctors told me the bone was broken," she says. "I was like, 'Oh, man.' But I never really looked at it too negatively. I don't think you can do that. In fact, I think the accident was good for me. It told me how much I love this sport."

It was a long road back for Sarah. In order to regain strength in her right leg, she participated in weight training, cycling, and yoga seven days a week. When the 1999–2000 World Cup competitions rolled around, Sarah was ready. She posted eleven "top–twenty" finishes that year. In 2000–2001 Schleper did even better. In the 2001 competitions, she snatched up four World Cup "top–ten" finishes, including a second-place finish in slalom on December 12, 2000, in Sestriere, Italy, and a third-place finish in the giant slalom on December 30, 2000, in Semmering, Austria.

Daron Rahlves

Pronunciation: DAYR-in RAWLVZ
Birth date: June 12, 1973
Birthplace: Walnut Creek, California
Country: United States
Residence: Truckee, California
Height: 5'9" (175 cm)
Weight: 175 lbs. (79 kg)

At the Nagano Games in 1998, Daron posted the best finish for the U.S. men in both the super-G and giant slalom, finishing twentieth and seventh respectively. Then he surprised everyone in the 2001 World Championships in St. Anton, Austria, by winning the super-G world title, defeating Austrians Stephan Eberharter and Hermann Maier. Now he holds three U.S. national titles: two in the giant slalom (1995, 1996) and one in the super-G (2000).

Daron became the first American man since Bill Johnson to win back-to-back World Cup races in March of 2000. At a weekend competition in Kvitfjell, Norway, he blew everyone away with two downhill golds in two days.

After the twin wins, retired Olympian Kitt advised Daron to find out what gets him in the zone because that is what would sustain him when the emotional high was gone. Daron trained in the slalom (the same thing Kitt did before he skied his best downhill). Daron also gained insight about the downhill from Tommy Moe, the American 1994 Olympic downhill champion and super-G silver medalist.

Hermann Maier ▱━━━━━

Pronunciation: MY-er
Birth date: December 7, 1972
Birthplace: Flachau, Austria
Country: Austria
Residence: Flachau, Austria
Height: 5'11" (180 cm)
Weight: 195 lbs. (88 kg)

Hermann learned to ski at age three in his hometown of Flachau, Austria, home of the Atomic Ski Company. By age six, he had won a number of junior races. At fifteen, Maier attended the famed Austrian Ski Academy in Schladming but was sent home because of his slight build. He weighed just over one hundred pounds.

Returning to Flachau, Hermann began masonry school, and for the next six years, he spent his summers laying brick and his winters teaching others to ski at his parents' ski school. Then in October 1994, Hermann decided to compete in the professional ranks. "I still remember the date," he says. "I just said to myself, 'I have to try a career as a ski racer. I have to at least try.'"

Many agree that Hermann is the best men's alpine skier in the world. At the 1998 Olympic Games, Maier was involved in a violent crash in the downhill. Eighteen seconds into his run, while zooming sideways off a tight turn, he hung in the air for about thirty yards before crashing through two safety nets. Amazingly, Hermann was uninjured, coming to rest in several inches of fresh snow. He went on to win two gold medals. In all, eight of the top twenty men's downhillers crashed or missed a gate near the place where Hermann lost control.

At the 1998 Games, Hermann competed in four of five alpine events: downhill, super-G, giant slalom, and combined. He won gold in the super-G and a few days later, blew everyone away in the giant slalom to become the first Austrian man in forty-two years to win gold in that event. He was nicknamed "The Herminator" after his fellow countryman, Arnold Schwarzenegger, said on TV, "He is 'The Herminator,' and he'll be back."

Maier's younger brother, Alexander, competes in the 2002 Winter Olympic Games as a World Cup snowboarder.

Picabo Street

Pronunciation: PEEK-uh-boo
Birth date: April 3, 1971
Birthplace: Triumph, Idaho
Country: United States
Residence: Park City, Utah
Height: 5'7" (170 cm)
Weight: 161 lbs. (73 kg)

When Picabo was born, her parents, Stubby and Dee Street, decided their daughter should have the opportunity to choose her own name. For her first two years, they simply called her "Little Girl." The Street family lived in Triumph, Idaho, and a nearby town named Picabo captured Stubby's attention as he read about the Picabo Indian Tribe. When "Little Girl" was two years old, her mother took her to get a U.S. passport in preparation for a family trip to Mexico. Dee tried to convince the agent to put

"Little Girl" on her daughter's passport. Instead, the agent gave Dee and Stubby two weeks to come up with a real name for their daughter. During that time, Stubby was playing a game of peekaboo with his daughter when he remembered the name of the nearby town. Finally Stubby and Dee settled on Picabo, which means "shining waters." Two years later, Picabo's parents offered her the chance to change her name, but she declined.

Many people recognized Picabo's skiing ability at an early age, but most concluded that her lack of discipline would keep her from reaching her potential. At a U.S. dry-land camp in 1990, she was so weak and flabby that she was sent home. In Hawaii, where the family was living at the time, Picabo's father was building a wall around a friend's property and insisted that his daughter help. As she moved rock piles and mixed mud, Picabo learned that it felt good to work hard. She returned to the U.S. Ski Team with a new attitude. She went on to win a number of titles, including several Olympic medals.

Picabo Street makes her third Olympic appearance at the 2002 Games. Many Americans are familiar with her rise to international distinction after taking the silver medal in the downhill at the 1994 Lillehammer Games. In the 1998 games, Picabo overcame a severe knee injury to claim a gold medal in the super-G. She became only the fourth American woman to win two Olympic medals in alpine skiing. She has also won consecutive World Cup downhill titles (1995, 1996) and the downhill gold medal at the 1996 World Championships. She was the first American to win a World Cup championship in downhill.

After her amazing run at the 1998 Games, Picabo was involved in a crash that left her with a broken leg and a torn ligament in her right knee. Her injuries kept her from racing for thirty-three months, but she managed to fight her way back in time for the World Cup competition in Val d'Isere, France, on December 6, 2000. Though she finished thirty-fourth in the race, she proved that she's back and ready for more.

Christian Athletes in Skiing

Tasha Nelson

Birth date: July 1, 1974
Birthplace: Mound, Minnesota
Country: United States
Residence: Mound, Minnesota
Height: 5'7-1/2" (168 cm)
Weight: 150 lbs. (68 kg)

Tasha Nelson grew up skiing at Buck Hill. At the age of eight, she joined Erich Sailer's racing program and began competing. She graduated from Stratton Mountain School and continued to race, but when she was eighteen, injuries to her left knee kept her off the slopes for three consecutive seasons

(1992–94), almost derailing her career. After her recovery, Tasha fought back, winning the 1996 North American Slalom title and earning a place on the U.S. Ski Team.

Tasha was twenty-one years old before she earned the right to compete in the World Cup, an elite competition that includes only the best skiers in the world. Tasha was one of the top four U.S. skiers.

In 1998, Tasha qualified for the U.S. Olympic Team. Although she failed to medal, just being in the Olympic village and associating with the top athletes in the world fulfilled a dream for her. Seeing the burning desire to win that drove her fellow athletes motivated her to do her very best.

Tasha considers herself a "slalom specialist," so she now competes only in the slalom, though in the past she has also competed in many other events, especially the giant slalom.

What is it like to careen down an alpine slalom course? Tasha loves the turns and twists, but the ultimate thrill for her is just being there. "I remember standing at the top of the course," she says, "looking down the mountain and thinking, *This is it. This is the Olympics. Give it all you got.*"

She did give it all she had, and even though she fell, Tasha knew she had done her best.

Tasha says that the starting gate was her favorite part of the Olympic competition. "In the starting gate, there's a little starter on each side," she says. "Your coach is right next to you. There are cameras all over the place. When you get into the starting gate, there's a camera showing the contestant [before you] going down the mountain. Your heart is going like two hundred beats a minute and you're thinking, *This is the Olympics. This is one of the greatest moments of my life. I'm competing at the highest level I can compete on. I'm qualified for this.* You get tingles. But you have to focus. You focus on what you need to do—your run—what the first few gates will be like."

Tasha says that once you're on the course, you no longer think about it. "You can try to memorize it—every turn and section—but going at breakneck speed makes you forget all the details. You simply see a couple gates ahead and go with it."

Tasha remembers the finish line in the Olympics. "People are lining the course from top to bottom," she says. "There's a big crowd at the bottom. People have these cowbells, and they're ringing them and cheering, and you're right in the middle of it."

Competing in the Olympic Games was an amazing experience for Tasha. But her family and those who gave her support and encouragement as she grew in her skills are the focus of her life. Even the Olympic Games can't compete with her love and commitment to them.

"It all goes to my support group: my family, my parents and my brothers, and my coaches," Tasha says. "Erich Sailor is my coach. He has coached me since I was eight years old. He brought me up in the sport. I was one of the hardest workers, but I wasn't always the most talented. I'd always be out there training. He believed in me. He'd say, 'You're going to make it. You're going to be in the Olympics.' He knew I could do it. He'd always pick out the best parts of my skiing and work on my strengths. He'd point out the weaknesses. But he majored on my strengths."

As Tasha struggled to overcome her injuries, Rob Clayton became one of the most influential people in her life. "I had some knee injuries and surgery on my knees a few years ago. Rob was my coach after those surgeries. He worked with me for three years to help me get back to it. He would tell me, 'You're going to win today.' He'd tell me what to focus on, and he always knew what buttons to push. If he knew making me mad would make me go faster, he'd get me mad."

Even though Tasha has different coaches on the World Cup circuit, Erich Sailor and Rob Clayton continue to stay in touch and encourage her to do her best. Tasha says, "Today, if I'm in Europe, I'll call them and talk, and they'll encourage me."

Tasha is one of only a few athletes on the circuit who maintains a Christian testimony—a key element of her success. "I know my Christian story isn't that exciting because I grew up in a Christian home," she says with a laugh. "We went to church and Sunday school every Sunday, and Bible study and prayer on Wednesday nights. We prayed with our parents every night and before we ate and had Bible time. Everything we did revolved around our relationship with Jesus.

"At a young age, I accepted Jesus into my heart, but I don't remember most of the details except that it happened. I was in the car, and we were driving home from church. I was about six. My brothers and I were all sitting in the back, and I kind of announced, 'I'm ready to accept Jesus into my heart.' My parents just led me in the prayer while we were driving down the road."

It was when Tasha began to race at the age of eight, mostly in USSA (United States Ski Association) races, that her faith began to make an impact on her life. She specialized in slalom and giant slalom. And she was a winner—taking almost every race. "At fifteen, I started participating in world competitions and racing in Europe—slalom and giant slalom, North American series races and Europa Cup," she says.

"When I was in ninth grade, I went out for the ski team. That was when I really began to shine as a Christian. It was there you could see the contrast between the way I believed and the way others did, especially on the road. I always put God first and would read the Bible on the bus. Kids would come up to me and say, 'Hey, read me something from that.' Later, I would get letters from athletes I'd met and they'd say, 'I always remember you reading the Bible, and now I've accepted Jesus into my heart. I'm really on fire, and you had an influence on that.'"

During this time, Tasha learned a special kind of boldness that came from living her faith before the world.

"I wasn't telling people about Jesus, but it was just my actions which were the real boldness," she says. "The contrast between the environment I was in in school and then at home was tremendous. I would pray before I'd eat and people would ask, 'What are you doing?' So a lot of my boldness was in my actions."

How does her faith impact her skiing? Tasha feels it's been mostly in the area of attitude. "I'd ski in the race and have to trust God to help me do my best and leave the results to him," she says. "That's impacted my teammates a lot because I might have a bad race, but I wouldn't really get down or mad. I'd just say, 'I'm trusting God. I'll be back.' People wouldn't see me get really negative on life."

Tasha's favorite Bible verse is Romans 8:28: "We know that in all things God works for the good of those who love him, who have been called according to his purpose."

Tasha says, "I know that no matter what I go through, I can trust God for victory. It's going to come out in the end for the best, for what he wanted. If I give it my all, I'll see God work things out."

How does Tasha apply this principle to her sport? "There have been world competitions where I've fallen or didn't get back for a second run. So I'd just talk to the Lord and trust him that if he wanted me to be victorious, he'd help me win. Maybe there was something more that I needed to learn. My coach and others would ask, 'Don't you get down?' And I just say, 'No, I think attitude determines altitude.' I'm always trying to put positive things into my mind, and that keeps my eyes on God."

What does Tasha like to tell young people when she speaks to them about her life, her skiing, and her faith? "What you put into life, you're going to get out of life," she says. "You put passion into your life, you'll have a passionate life. If you believe in yourself and believe in God and trust him for the results, he'll lead you. You'll be happy and satisfied."

She tells others, "Ultimately, never give up. I had three knee injuries. It started in December one year, then I'd recover by March, train all summer, and then get injured in the fall. The next year it happened in December and the one after that in November. It was heartbreaking. The only reason I came back was because I knew I had the potential to win and God would get me there. So I'd tell myself, 'Never give up. Winners never give up.'

"Galatians 6:9 was real influential at the time: 'Let us not become weary in doing good, for at the proper time we will reap a harvest if we do not give up.' That one really encouraged me."

Today, Tasha is in the best shape of her life and confident as she competes for a spot on the U.S. Olympic Team. No one knows what lies ahead. But one thing is sure: Tasha Nelson will give her best— to her country, to her sport, and to her God.

Caroline Lalive ▭━▭━▭━▭━▬

> Birth date: August 10, 1979
> Birthplace: Steamboat Springs, Colorado
> Country: United States
> Residence: Steamboat Springs, Colorado
> Height: 5'5" (163 cm)
> Weight: 137 lbs. (62.3 kg)

At the 1998 Olympics in Nagano, Caroline took seventh place in the combined, the best any U.S. woman has done in the event in the Olympics in more than fifty years. Then in 1999, she scored World Cup points in four events—slalom, giant slalom, super-G, and downhill. She is considered one of the best American women on the circuit as a generalist. In 2000 she scored in all five alpine events, and reached the podium for the first time for the combined. She was the 1999 World Juniors champion and plans to build on recent victories that are improving her multi-event rankings.

Caroline was raised in a Christian family. She made her decision to trust Jesus at about age eight in the backseat of a visiting missionary's car. "The missionaries were visiting our church in Lake Tahoe, California," she says. "They weren't skiers, but we were all going to lunch. I rode in the back of their car. The wife just asked me if I wanted to pray to receive Christ. I was so young, but I said yes. I got baptized shortly after that in Lake Tahoe."

For Caroline, growing up in a Christian home seemed normal and natural. She wasn't really aware of the differences her faith would make in her life until she reached the age of fourteen. "That was when it became a reality," she says. "I began traveling on my own for skiing. I saw the importance of being a Christian in that secular world. It was so different—what kids were into. At that time, I made a real commitment, because I think I had begun to really get it. Skiing is a very secular sport. At age fourteen, I was rushed into the throes of everything. I realized I needed to make [my faith] more real or I'd lose it."

How has knowing Christ helped Caroline on the skiing circuit?

"I have a peace knowing God is ultimately in control day to day," she says. "I can remember as a little girl, before racing, always praying and asking the Lord to be with me. I grew up feeling like the Lord had really blessed me with this talent. He was my confidence. I knew he was with me and that gave me strength, even for races."

As Caroline continued to ski, the competition became fiercer. And Caroline drew even closer to the Lord. "I draw my strength from the Lord all the time. When a day doesn't go well, I know God is faithful. Knowing I've got the Creator of the universe on my side is incredible. When I was little, I would say to my dad, 'Can you imagine if Jesus skied how awesome he would be?' There's a lot of joy having Christ in my life. It gives me joy in spite of hard and frustrating times."

Caroline's coach, George Capaul, says about his student, "Caroline's grown very progressively—she's loaded, ready to do more, knows the circuit, and when she can, she lets it rip."

What are some of Caroline's great moments in skiing?

"My first huge experience was the Olympics," she says. "I finished seventh. I didn't really expect anything. It was the best female American finish in that event in fifty years. It gave me a glimmer of what the future could hold."

What was it like to be in Japan?

"Well, I was eighteen. I had no expectations. It was more just to gain experience. It was my first time racing in Japan. Culturally, it's very different. The people were so warm and so excited to have the Olympics there. And if you had blonde hair, they all wanted your autograph. They even wanted my mom's autograph. She's blonde. We ate fish every day for three weeks. It was crazy, but fun."

Caroline confessed that she really hadn't felt that strong in the combined, but she always prayed with her parents before a race and that, she believes, helped greatly in her amazing seventh-place finish.

Caroline says that singing is one of her success secrets. "I like to sing while I'm going down the slope," she says. "In the downhill, when you're in a tuck for thirty seconds, I'd just sing my way through it. What do I sing? Do you remember Psalty? He sang this song 'Climbing My Mountain.' So I sing that a lot. People think I'm a little nuts. 'Hey, there's this ski racer out there singing Psalty on the way down,' they say. But it encourages me."

Another highlight of her career was becoming the World Junior champion. "Hearing the National Anthem, standing on the podium," she says, "and receiving the gold was something really exciting and beautiful. That was in 1999.

"Then, last year I was second in the World Cup and ended up finishing the season second in the world. I'm just kind of making my way up there hoping for the gold medal spot."

Caroline's source of strength is the Bible and one of her favorite verses is 2 Timothy 4:7: "I have fought the good fight, I have finished the race, I have kept the faith."

"I have fought the good fight," she says. "I have finished the race and kept the faith. For me, especially in skiing, it's so important because if you make a mistake, you feel like you really blew it. And the skiing season is so long. Endurance is what it's all about. We only have four weeks off the whole year. You're always racing or training. You can have days that are really frustrating. That verse reminds me to keep fighting and keep the faith. It reminds me to hang in there, and keep my faith strong."

Another one of Caroline's favorite Bible verses is Philippians 1:6: "Being confident of this, that he who began a good work in you will carry it on to completion until the day of Christ Jesus."

One of the new things Caroline is doing before a race is reciting a verse of Scripture as she stands in the starting gate. "At the top of my course," she says, "I recite Scripture before I race. Usually, I try to have a new Scripture for each race. If you think about it, you're standing up there, getting ready to go eighty miles an hour down a course. Your nerves are sky high. So I would try to think of verses that would give me peace. Like 1 John 4:18: 'There is no fear in love. But perfect love drives out fear.' That one would calm my fears. Doing this Scripture thing gives me complete peace. It also gives me something that is exciting. I have a coach who's not even a Christian, and he's quoting Scripture with me, trying to get me fired up. Even though people might give you strange looks, it's powerful."

Who has been the most influential person in Caroline's life?

"When I was younger," she says, "I never had huge idols or heroes. Still, I think my family has been incredibly supportive of me. My dad is Swiss, and he taught me to ski before I was two. My mom knew nothing about skiing, but she brought me a lot of encouragement in skiing and racing. She's my rock, keeps me from losing my mind. My brother and sister too. My sister is a great snowboarder, and she was always so gracious to let me pave the way. She never tried to bring me down or acted with jealousy."

Caroline has also found great support in her Christian friends. "My Christian family is very generous with their prayers for me. Every time I race, I have people all over praying for me. We have a prayer chain in Steamboat Springs. It's a real lonely road on the women's circuit for Christians. So being in Europe for a couple months at a time with no Christian fellowship, those prayers are my lifeline. I have to attribute every bit of success I've had to them."

What advice does Caroline have for young people?

"One of the most important things is never lose sight of your dreams. When you have a dream, there's no guarantee the road will be easy. But the lessons you learn along the way and the rewards are so exciting. People often have huge dreams, but then reality kicks in and they give up on them. I think if you have a dream—if it's at all within your capability—you should go for it with everything you have. Remember that God is faithful. As long as he's in the number-one spot in your life, he will be there with you, doing everything to help you make it.

"I guess the main thing I'd say is when you're down, when things are going badly, remember that God has a greater plan for you, and he is going to work it out to help you be a better person and open up a greater future for you. I've had days when I was crying and completely discouraged, but, sure enough, down the road I was blessed again."

Those are good words for any athlete, and it's easy to see that Caroline has put them to work in her life.

Other Winter Olympic Sports

Cross-Country Skiing
Men:	Women:
10 kilometer	5 kilometer
15 kilometer	10 kilometer
30 kilometer	15 kilometer
50 kilometer	30 kilometer
40 kilometer relay	20 kilometer relay

Biathlon (cross-country skiing and shooting):
Men:	Women:
10 kilometer	7.5 kilometer
20 kilometer	15 kilometer
30 kilometer relay	30 kilometer relay

FREESTYLE SKIING

Doing tricks on skis is probably as old as skiing itself, going back more than five thousand years. But freestyle skiing is a uniquely American pastime. Catching fire in the 1960s, this thrilling mix of alpine skiing and acrobatics is now an Olympic sport.

The first freestyle skiing competition was held in 1966 in Attitash, New Hampshire, making a show of technical (required jumps and tricks) and freestyle (stylistic/personal) skills. Today, it's a high-flying daredevil event that has taken the sport by storm. "If you don't push the edge every time you ski, you ain't doing it!" one skier hyped.

The International Ski Federation (FIS) has tamed the wild side of freestyle, eliminating some of the more dangerous aspects and adding solid rules. The first World Cup series took place in 1980, and the first World Championships were held in 1986 in Tignes, France,

Photo by: Matthew Stockman / Allsport

featuring moguls (coming down a slope full of bumps), aerials (jumps and tricks in the air), and ballet (fluid, ballet-like movements).

Freestyle skiers first demonstrated their sport at the 1988 Winter Olympic Games in Calgary. As the sport grew in popularity, the International Olympic Committee (IOC) decided to add freestyle to the Olympic program in time for the Winter Games in Albertville, though they weren't ready to include aerials and ballet—only moguls were allowed.

In Albertville, the freestyle competitions were hugely popular and the IOC acted quickly, adding aerials to the Lillehammer program. Ballet has not yet been accepted in the Olympic program.

Freestyle skiing (various tricks performed on skis):
   Men's Moguls
   Men's Aerials
   Women's Moguls
   Women's Aerials

Olympic Watch

Eric Bergoust

Pronunciation: Eric BER-gust
Birth date: August 27, 1969
Birthplace: Missoula, Montana
Country: United States
Residence: Park City, Utah
Height: 6′ (183 cm)
Weight: 165 lbs. (75 kg)

Eric became the first 1998 Olympic gold medalist in aerials. And he holds the world record for the highest score in aerials. On August 13, 2000, at the World Cup competition in Mt. Buller, Australia, Eric earned an amazing 260.98 points. Nailing a double-full-full-full (four twists, three flips), he received 133.05 points for his first jump. In Australia, Italy, and at the Nagano Winter Olympic Games, Eric performed the three highest-scoring jumps in aerials history—truly the man to beat in 2002!

A Quick Look at Nordic Combined

Legendary Norwegian athlete Sondre Nordheim completed the first measured ski jump in 1860. Trysil, Norway, in 1862, hosted the first actual competition. Throughout the mid–1800s, ski carnivals featured ski jumping in Norway. The sport got a great boost when, in 1892, the Norwegian royal family awarded the King's Cup trophy to the ski-jumping winner at the annual meet in Holmenkollen.

Nordic Combined involves cross-country skiing, a 15-kilometer race, and also ski-jumping a 295-ft. hill. Norwegian immigrants brought the sport to the United States, where the first ski jumping meet there took place on February 8, 1887. Mikkel Hemmestvedt, a Norwegian, went home the winner.

Every Olympic Winter Games has included ski jumping. The large-hill competition began in 1924.

The individual normal-hill competition was added in 1964. The 1988 Calgary Games featured the first team competition.

   Norway ranks as the leader with twenty-four medals in ski jumping.

Combined Cross-Country and Jumping Events (Men only):
   Nordic Combined
   Team Nordic Combined

Olympic Watch

Todd Lodwick

Pronunciation: LAHD-wik
Birth date: November 21, 1976
Birthplace: Steamboat Springs, Colorado
Country: United States
Residence: Steamboat Springs, Colorado
Height: 5'9-1/2" (177 cm)
Weight: 144 lbs. (65 kg)

   Todd Lodwich has competed in the last two Olympic Games, where jumping was his strength in Nordic combined. Now cross-country skiing takes precedence. He finished thirteenth at Lillehammer in 1994. He helped the U.S. team finish seventh at Lillehammer. At the Nagano Games, he finished in twentieth place.

4

SNOWBOARDING

Whether it's skiing down a mountain on a board like a little surfboard or zigzagging across a "halfpipe" performing tricks like skateboarders do, snowboarding has caught on like wildfire in the United States and the world.

Snowboarding originated in the United States in the 1960s as people across the country began to seek out new wintertime activities. Many people point to Sherman Poppen as the inventor of the snowboard in 1965. Poppen wanted to build a skiing apparatus for his daughter by bracing a pair of skis together and tying a rope to the front to help her steer. Snowboarders were first called "snurfers," as the official snowboard came out in 1966 when surfing was popular. Surfers and skateboarders soon caught the fever, and by 1980 snowboarding had become a nationwide activity.

Photo by: Shaun Botterill / Allsport

Competitions began in the 1980s. The United States held the National Championships in 1982 and then hosted the World Championships in 1983. In 1987 a World Cup tour began.

Men's and women's snowboarding debuted at the 1998 Winter Olympics in Nagano, with alpine and freestyle events. It returns to the Salt Lake City Olympics with two men's and two women's events. The alpine event is no longer a traditional giant slalom but a parallel giant slalom that lets snowboarders go head-to-head in an exciting elimination format. The halfpipe, an event performed inside a u-shaped track that resembles the bottom half of a large pipe, returns as the freestyle event.

Snowboarding:
> **Men's Giant Slalom**
> **Men's Halfpipe**
> **Women's Giant Slalom**
> **Women's Halfpipe**

Olympic Watch

Tricia Byrnes

Birth date: November 18, 1974
Birthplace: Greenwich, Connecticut
Country: United States
Residence: New Canaan, Connecticut
Height: 5'7" (170 cm)
Weight: 146 lbs. (66 kg)

Though snowboarding debuted at the 1998 Nagano Winter Games, Tricia Byrnes failed to qualify for the U.S. Snowboarding Team. But she quickly recovered and has established herself as a premier halfpipe rider. In 1999 she won seven World Cup events, securing the halfpipe World Cup title.

Chris Klug

Birth date: November 18, 1972
Birthplace: Vail, Colorado
Country: United States
Residence: Aspen, Colorado
Height: 6'2" (188 cm)
Weight: 207 lbs. (94 kg)

In 2000 Chris Klug discovered he had the same liver disease that killed former NFL great Walter Payton. He needed a liver transplant to save his life. In July of that year, he got a transplant and was soon back on the World Cup circuit. He won his first World Cup race in January, 2001—a parallel giant slalom in Italy.

Chris is now the top American alpine snowboarder. He has three World Cup wins. At the 1998 Nagano Winter Games, he finished a great first run, but a poor second run put him in second place.

5

FIGURE SKATING

Considered the most-watched sport in the world today, figure skating ranks as a highlight of the Winter Olympic Games. Winners go on to long careers in professional skating the world over.

The origins of the sport seem to point back to a time when warriors and hunters honed skates from reindeer antlers or elk bones. It wasn't until much later that blades were forged from iron and steel. In the sixteenth century, skaters moved material goods and food across the many frozen waterways of Europe.

When artisans learned to craft skates with iron and steel blades, skating suddenly became something to do for fun. In the 1600s, the Dutch wore skates as they traveled along frozen canals, visiting home-to-home and town-to-town. They learned the "Dutch Roll," the simple maneuver learned by all skaters that involves pushing off

Photo by: Darren England / Allsport

one skate and gliding on the other. Later, the French dandied it up with pirouettes and spins.

In 1892 the International Skating Union (ISU) was founded. Figure skating was added to the Summer Olympics in 1908, because it could be held indoors. But in 1924, it officially became a Winter Olympics sport. Singles and pairs events debuted in the Summer Games of 1920 and were transferred to the Winter Olympics the next go-round. Ice dancing appeared at the 1976 Olympics at Innsbruck.

The United States has fared well in the sport of figure skating, winning more medals than any other nation, a total of forty (twelve gold, thirteen silver, and fifteen bronze). The United States is particularly strong in ladies' singles and has won more than a third of the event's medals since 1924.

FEBRUARY 20 1988 — On This Day In Olympic History

They called it "the battle of the Brians" as Brian Boitano of the United States and Brian Orser of Canada skated it out for the men's singles figure-skating title. In the end, Boitano came out on top.

Figure skating:
> **Men's Singles**
> **Women's Singles**
> **Pairs**
> **Ice Dancing**

Great Figure Skaters of the Past

Dick Button

Born in Englewood, New Jersey, in 1929, Dick Button grew into a chubby twelve-year-old. As his interest in figure skating grew, people said he would never be a champion because of his weight. But he slimmed down, entered competitions at age thirteen, and began to win. In 1946 Dick won the first of seven titles in the USFSC (United States Figure Skating Championships). In 1948 he won the first of five world championships. Today many hear him commentate figure-skating events at the Olympics. But at one time, he was the man to beat—a real figure-skating legend.

The 1948 Olympics in St. Moritz, Switzerland, the first Games to take place after World War II, promised to be the world event of the decade. People streamed from all over the world to see this grand snowy event.

Dick Button was ready. A freshman at Harvard College, he wanted to try something new. He could play it safe and possibly win the gold. But something else in him pushed him to want to move the sport to new heights of athleticism. His dream: performing the first double axel in Olympic and international competition.

Two days before his scheduled free skate, Dick completed the feat in practice. Executed by leaping from the outside edge of the skate while going forward, the skater must rotate two and a half times and come down on the other foot going backward. No one had ever seen it performed successfully in competition.

Dick knew he had to try it, even if he failed.

FEBRUARY 19 1928 — On This Day In Olympic History

A pioneer of graceful moves, artful jumps, and all-round beauty of style and appearance on the ice, Sonja Henie, fifteen, of Norway, won the gold in figure skating. She would go on to win two more medals in the next two Olympics. No other woman has won three medals in a row in singles figure skating.

But he didn't fail. He completed the double axel to thunderous applause. Eight of the nine judges ranked him in first place, and he recorded the highest point total ever for the gold medal.

Many thought he would turn pro right then and there, but Dick had three more years of school to complete—and other dreams—maybe even another gold medal.

The 1952 Olympics in Oslo, Norway, seemed a little tamer than the last, but Dick had a new move he wanted to showcase—a triple jump, called a loop.

He prepared well. He knew he had it down. Then at the last second, in the middle of his routine, he forgot which shoulder went forward!

Years of practice, though, and steady nerves took over. He remembered at the last second and performed the triple loop perfectly. Again, the crowd roared, and the nine judges unanimously awarded Dick Button the gold medal.

He turned professional after that Olympics, and through the years, has provided television commentary for countless figure skating events. When the United States Olympic Hall of Fame was created in 1983, Dick Button was inducted as a member of the first class.

Peggy Fleming

Peggy Fleming's career debut as a figure skater was punctuated by tragedy. Her coach, Billy Kipp, and eighteen members of the U.S. Skate Team were killed in a plane crash in 1961. Only thirteen years old at the time, Peggy has dedicated her life to honoring her former coach and the guidance he brought to her life.

Peggy won her first U.S. National Championship at age fifteen and went on to win four more in consecutive years. In 1964 she placed sixth in singles figure skating at the Innsbruck (Austria) Olympic Games.

In 1966 Peggy won the first of three World Championships in her sport, becoming a favorite for the 1968 Games in Grenoble, France. She combined careful and flawless understanding of the compulsories with a grace on ice in freeskating that stunned viewers. When it was her turn to perform

FEBRUARY
3
1956

On This Day In Olympic History

The pairs figure-skating judges gave a low score to a German pair competing in the Olympic Games in Cortina D'Ampezzo, Italy. The crowd was so enraged that they pelted the judges with oranges.

Erik Schlopy of the USA in action during the men's giant slalom World Cup event in Adelboden, Switzerland.

Photo by: Zoom Sports / Allsport

Tricia Byrnes #16 of the USA jumps as she grabs her board in the Women's Halfpipe Event during World Cup Snowboarding at Mountain Village in Park City, Utah.

Photo by: Elsa Hasch / Allsport

Anne Abernathy (ISV), 20th in Women's Luge at the 1994 Winter Olympics in Lillehammer.

Photo by: Clive Brunskill / Allsport

Sonja Henie of Norway in action during the Figure Skating event at the 1924 Winter Olympic Games in Chamonix, France. Henie finished in eighth place.

Photo by: IOC Olympic Museum / Allsport

Silver medal winner Todd Eldredge of the USA jumps during the men's free skating program at the 2001 World Figure Skating Championships at the GM Place in Vancouver, Canada.

Photo by: Brian Bahr / Allsport

Eric Heiden of the USA rounds a turn during the
1980 Winter Olympics in Lake Placid, New York.

Photo by: Tony Duffy / Allsport

Gianni Romme of the Netherlands skates to a gold medal in the men's 5,000-meter speed skating event during the 1998 Winter Olympic Games in Nagano, Japan. Romme set a new world record with a time of 6:22:00.

Photo by: Doug Pensinger / Allsport

USA hockey team players hug and celebrate on the ice after defeating Finland to win the gold medal game of the 1980 Winter Olympics in Lake Placid, New York.

Photo by: Steve Powell / Allsport

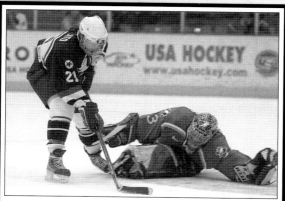

Cammi Granato #21 of the USA takes a shot on Kim St. Pierre #33 of Canada during the Women's World Hockey Championships at Mariucci Arena in Minneapolis, Minnesota. Canada defeated the USA 3-2 to win the gold medal

Photo by: Elsa Hasch / Allsport

Mark Grimmette and Brian Martin of the USA in action during the two-man luge event in which they won bronze at the Winter Olympic Games in Nagano, Japan.

Vonnetta Flowers and Bonny Warner of USA-2 (from left) Jean Racine and Jennifer Davidson of USA-1 and Jill Bakken and Kristi McGihon of USA-3 finished second, first, and third respectively in the women's bobsleigh event during the Park City World Cup at Utah Olympic Park in Park City, Utah.

the four-minute program, she floated and spiraled across the ice as if she were walking on air. Like a prima donna ballerina, she entranced the crowd and pushed women's figure skating to new levels of grace and perfection. All the judges agreed she had won the gold medal—one of the few unanimous decisions in such an event in Olympic history.

The plane crash that killed her coach and fellow skaters could have sidelined Peggy's career as well. But her love for her coach and commitment to the sport of figure skating sped her on. Her new coach, Carlo Fassi, who would go on to guide many great names in the sport, rebuilt the team. With Peggy as its centerpiece, American figure skating rose to new heights and greater glory than ever before.

Dorothy Hamill

Dorothy Hamill never won a World Championship prior to skating in the Olympics. She wasn't a flashy skating icon like Peggy Fleming. But she possessed other qualities, such as personal creativity on the ice and a joyous skating style that mesmerized crowds. Today, the Hamill camel, invented by Dorothy, remains an often-displayed part of a complete skating program.

At the 1976 Winter Olympics in Innsbruck, Dorothy remained far from a favorite. She'd won two U.S. National Championships, but other skaters such as Christine Errath of East Germany and

Dianne de Leeuw of the Netherlands were considered the skaters to watch.

Dorothy's coach, Carlo Fassi, had also coached such greats as Peggy Fleming. But Dorothy was a very different type of skater. While Fleming was all grace and fluttery ballet movements, Dorothy was a gymnast of the ice. She leaped, pirouetted, and spun with a degree of excellence that spectators and judges had not seen before.

And something else made Dorothy unique. She lacked the financial backing available to other skaters. A friend had sewn together the pink knit dress she wore in the competition, and her father recorded the melodies from *Seahawk*, a movie with Errol Flynn that accompanied her performance on ice.

Dorothy wheeled about the ice like a race car driver. She performed axels, high-speed spins, and concluded her program with her signature move, the Hamill camel. Here, her high-speed standing spin sank into a sit spin that brought lengthy applause from the audience.

Her marks: 5.8s and 5.9s for artistry. No one was surprised when the gold medal became hers a few skaters later.

Scott Hamilton

Scott Hamilton didn't have a great start in life. Adopted into a loving family, he suffered a serious setback at five years of age—his body simply stopped growing. Unable to absorb nutrients from the food he ate, he quickly became malnourished. No one seemed to know why. Various doctors proposed solutions, but Scott didn't improve.

For the next four years, Scott was taken from hospital to hospital, doctor to doctor, without discovering the reason for his condition. Then at age nine, he tagged along with his sister to the skating rink and decided he wanted to try it.

Many tears and falls later, Scott realized he had a talent for skating. And something else happened—he began to grow again. The condition had disappeared the same way it had appeared—without warning and without explanation. Today Scott says, "I skated myself out of it."

FEBRUARY 21 1992

On This Day In Olympic History

No one had won a gold medal in women's singles figure skating for the United States since Dorothy Hamill claimed the title in 1976. Today, Kristi Yamaguchi added her name to the record books with a first-place finish.

Scott tried ice hockey first, but his small stature made him a target for pummeling by defensemen. Soon, he turned to figure skating. A coach helped him develop in that arena, and he won his first U.S. Men's Junior Championship in 1976.

Things were looking great until the Hamiltons realized they did not have the money to support Scott in college and in his career as a figure skater. Seeing his potential, however, Carlo Fassi, the same coach who had worked with Dorothy Hamill and Peggy Fleming, stepped in. He found someone to sponsor Scott, and the great adventure was back on track.

Scott excelled and grew, placing well in various competitions. At the 1980 Winter Olympic Games, he performed six triples, whirling and spinning like a dervish on the ice. He placed fifth overall.

Scott, nicknamed "Rocky" now because he always skated to the theme from the movie *Rocky*, was considered a contender—but not number one. David Santee was the American favorite at national events during the 1981–1983 seasons. Scott began moving up, though, and took first in the World Championships in 1981, successfully defending his title right up to the 1984 Olympic Games in Sarajevo, Yugoslavia.

Scott entered the 1984 Olympics with three World Championships behind him. It should have been an easy victory, but a cold led to an ear infection that disrupted Scott's balance. He performed well on the ice but felt sick. He didn't tell anyone what was going on, though, until after the competition.

Scott had never been good at the compulsories, drawing figures on the ice. But this time, he led in all of them—a virtual miracle.

In the short program, he also performed well. But the free skate was flawed. Scott had several mistakes and felt he had not done his best. He was almost certain he had lost the gold medal to Canadian Brian Orser, who was judged best in the free skate by eight of the nine judges. But he was surprised and gratified to learn that the judges had given him the gold based on his excellence in the other parts of the competition.

Scott told no one about the ear infection until the Olympics were over—a true competitor and a true man of character.

Olympic Watch

Michelle Kwan

Pronunciation: KWAHN
Birth date: July 7, 1980
Birthplace: Torrance, California
Country: United States
Residence: Los Angeles, California
Height: 5'2" (157 cm)
Weight: 110 lbs. (50 kg)

Michelle has been a top figure skater for the past six years. She has won three World Championships, five national titles, and an Olympic silver medal (in 1998). She even beat Tara Lipinski in the 1998 National Championships, though Lipinski recovered and skated so well at Nagano that she won the gold.

Since Nagano, Kwan has won two more world titles. She enrolled at UCLA for the 1999–2000 academic year so she could retreat from the rigors of Olympic stardom and lead a normal life.

Todd Eldredge

Birth date: August 28, 1971
Birthplace: Chatham, Massachusetts
Country: United States
Residence: Bloomfield Hills, Michigan
Height: 5'8" (173 cm)
Weight: 146 lbs. (66 kg)

Todd is no newcomer to the field. He has competed in seven World Championships and medaled five times, highlighted by a gold at the 1996 World Championships in Edmonton, Canada. He has also won five U.S. National Championship titles.

Todd decided to step away from amateur competitions in 1998 to participate in professional and exhibition events that would not disturb his Olympic eligibility. Now he returns to competition for the Salt Lake City Olympic Games. At the 2001 U.S. Championships in Boston, he took the silver and qualified for the World Championships in Vancouver, Canada. The only thing he lacks is an Olympic medal.

SPEED SKATING

Speed skating around a rink has existed since the first known competition in England on February 4, 1763. Other events and competitions sprang up until the first official meets were held in 1863 in Oslo, Norway.

The Netherlands hosted the first World Championships in 1889, with Dutch, Russian, American, and English athletes competing.

The sport was featured as a primary event at the first Winter Olympics in 1924 and has been included on the program ever since. Though at first only men raced, in 1960, four women's speed-skating events were held at Squaw Valley. The women's 5,000 meters was added to the program in Calgary in 1988. Ten events will be held in the 2002 Winter Olympic Games in Salt Lake City.

Photo by: Darren England / Allsport

Speed Skating:
   Men:
      500 meter
      1,000 meter
      1,500 meter
      5,000 meter
      10,000 meter
   Women:
      500 meter
      1,000 meter
      1,500 meter
      3,000 meter
      5,000 meter

FEBRUARY 10 1992

On This Day In Olympic History

For the first time a woman won a gold medal in two successive Olympics. The winner was Bonnie Blair in the 500-meter speed-skating event. On February 23, 1994, she would go on to win a fifth gold medal in the 1,000-meter race. No other American woman has won as many.

Olympic Speed Skaters of the Past

Eric Heiden

Since Eric Heiden sped away with five gold medals at the 1980 Winter Olympics in Lake Placid, New York, no other athlete has won that many medals in one Winter Olympics. Heiden's "show" lasted the full two weeks of the Games, as he dazzled fans and onlookers. Only Hjalmar Andersen of Norway showed the same spirit in 1952 when he swept the three long-distance speed-skating races at the Games in Helsinki. Ard Schenk of the Netherlands finished with similar honors in 1972. But Heiden's achievement was unique—no one had ever won in every race.

Eric was born June 14, 1958, and learned to skate shortly after learning to walk. He trained early in bicycling, running, and weightlifting.

Just twenty-one when he competed at Lake Placid, he was still a premed college student from Wisconsin. His sister, Beth, a year younger, also medaled at the Games, making it a family affair.

Eric quickly won the 500, 1,000, 1,500, and 5,000 meters, setting world and Olympic records along the way. The next day he drove, pushed, and skated the 10,000 meters (6.2 miles) like he had been set afire. He wiped out the field six seconds under the world record time.

Winning the five golds made Eric a hero to millions. He ended up turning down all kinds of commercial offers, saying, "Put my face on a cereal box? No thanks. I didn't get into skating to be famous. If I had, I would have played hockey."

Eric later participated in bicycling competitions, but did not see the level of success he had achieved in speed skating.

Chris Witty

Bonnie Blair won five gold medals over three Olympics, in 1988, 1992, and 1994. When the 1998 Olympics arrived, Bonnie had retired, and few gave the American team much notice.

They should have—they had overlooked a hard-driver named Chris Witty.

FEBRUARY 23 1980

On This Day In Olympic History

Five gold medals! That's how Eric Heiden finished today with a win in the speed-skating events. He became the first athlete to win five gold medals at a single Olympics.

Chris grew up in West Allis, Wisconsin. She started skating at twelve years of age, using a pair of rusty, too-large skates. She couldn't afford better. Her father had lost his job when the Allis-Chalmers plant closed down. Somehow the family scrimped along on Mrs. Witty's salary, buying Chris lessons in skating. She almost gave up, but then someone sent Chris a pair of new skates. At eighteen, she skated for the U.S. Olympic Skate Team at the 1994 Winter Olympic Games in Lillehammer, placing twenty-third.

Chris was just beginning to shine. When 1998 rolled around, she was well prepared, having built her endurance through running, skating, and body building. The Winter Games in Nagano, Japan, looked promising.

In the 1,500 meters, Chris surprised everyone with a bronze medal in the difficult event. She skated a 1:58:97, almost one second better than the American record. Marianne Timer of the Netherlands, though, took the gold with a 1:57:58 finish.

Chris knew that two days later, she would skate her best event, the 1,000 meters.

She held her curves, skated furiously, and looked like the best on ice that day. But Timmer took the gold again, and Chris had to settle for a silver medal.

Her father had been out of work for eight years. But that year, he found a full-time job. He and Chris's mother watched their daughter win the silver and bronze before cheering crowds.

Olympic Watch

Gianni Romme

Pronunciation: Johnny ROH-muh
Birth date: February 12, 1973
Birthplace: Lage Zwaluwe, Netherlands
Country: Netherlands
Residence: Uithoorn, Netherlands
Height: 6'3" (191 cm)
Weight: 190 lbs. (86 kg)

Gianni Romme rules long-distance speed skating. He holds three world records (3,000, 5,000, and 10,000 meters) and two Olympic gold medals (5,000 and 10,000 meters), having set two of the world records in Calgary.

FEBRUARY 18 1994

On This Day In Olympic History

You just have to keep trying! And that's what Dan Jansen did in the 1,000-meter speed-skating event. He failed to win a medal in the three previous Olympics. But today he won the gold.

Romme skated for the first time on double-bladed skates when he was five years of age. At thirteen, he began skating with serious enthusiasm, but he lacked coordination and concentration and didn't make the Dutch team till he was twenty-two. In 1995, he won a spot on the national team.

Jennifer Rodriguez

Birth date: June 8, 1976
Birthplace: Miami, Florida
Country: United States
Residence: Park City, Utah
Height: 5'4-1/2" (164 cm)
Weight: 126 lbs. (57 kg)

Jennifer Rodriguez began skating in Miami, a strange spot for a speed skater to debut. But she actually gained her first success on roller skates. She won twelve World Championship medals in roller skating, and was the only athlete to win World Championship medals in both artistic roller skating (similar to figure skating) and speed roller skating. She was awarded the 1991–92 U.S. Roller Skating Athlete of the Year.

Her fiancé, fellow U.S. speed skater K. C. Boutiette, encouraged her to try speed skating, but she didn't try it until late in 1995. Jennifer soon became one the nation's best speed skaters. She competed in her first all-around U.S. Championships in 1997, taking fourth. At the Winter Olympic Games in

Nagano, she qualified for four events—the 1,000, 1,500, 3,000, and 5,000 meter—winning a fourth place in the 3,000. She gained her first U.S. all-around title in 2000.

A Quick Look at Short-Track Speed Skating

Speed skating, featuring two skaters racing each other down the track, has always been a major feature of the Winter Olympic Games. However, short-track speed skating contains a whole new dynamic. It combines the element of speed with more than two enthusiastic competitors careening around a short oval track, each in search of a gold medal.

Short-track speed skating began in Europe soon after speed skating took hold as an international sport. Taking notice in the early 1900s, the United States and Canada featured competitions as early as 1906.

The sport grew in popularity during the twenties and thirties. But it wasn't until the 1988 Winter Games in Calgary that short track was added to the demonstration program. It featured ten events. In 1992 it was made an Olympic event with one individual and one relay event for men and for women. In 1994 it was expanded to six events in Lillehammer.

Short-Track Speed Skating:
- Men's 500 meter
- Men's 1,000 meter
- Men's 5,000 meter relay
- Women's 500 meter
- Women's 1,000 meter
- Women's 3,000 meter relay

ICE HOCKEY

The British introduced the sport of ice hockey to North America. Soldiers stationed in Nova Scotia, Canada, engaged in the earliest games. In the 1870s, a group of college students at McGill University in Montreal began running games and developed a set of rules to govern the sport. The "McGill Rules" stipulated the use of a puck rather than a rubber ball and set the team size at nine players.

In 1885, the Amateur Hockey Association of Canada, the first national hockey association, was organized in Montreal. A league of four teams was formed in Ontario, and the number of players per team was reduced from nine to seven.

The sport appeared in the United States in the 1890s. Games were first scheduled between Johns Hopkins and Yale Universities in 1895. The United States jumped ahead of Canada by organizing the first professional league. The Pro Hockey League formed in Houghton, Michigan, and gathered teams and players from Canada and the United States. The league folded, but in 1910 the National Hockey League was formed.

At the 1920 Summer Olympic Games, ice hockey was included for the first time as an Olympic sport. By 1924 it had been transferred to the Winter Games. Women's hockey became part of the Olympic Winter Games program in Nagano in 1998.

Canada and the Soviet Union have dominated throughout the history of Olympic ice hockey. The two countries hold fourteen of the nineteen Olympic golds.

FEBRUARY 22 1980 — On This Day In Olympic History

Some called it "the miracle on ice." Today, the American Olympic hockey team defeated the all-powerful Soviet Union team in Lake Placid, New York. The Americans trailed 3–2 in the last quarter, but turned things around by scoring two quick goals to win, 4–3. This wasn't even the gold-medal round. The Americans would take that against the Finns two days later. It became the first gold medal for the United States since 1960.

The U.S. Women's Ice Hockey Team took gold at the Nagano Winter Olympic Games, with Canada claiming the silver.

Ice Hockey (team sport):
  Men's
  Women's

Olympic Watch

Cammi Granato

Pronunciation: grah-NAH-toh
Birth date: March 25, 1971
Birthplace: Downers Grove, Illinois
Country: United States
Residence: Montreal, Quebec
Height: 5'7" (170 cm)
Weight: 140 lbs. (64 kg)

As captain of the 1998 U.S. Women's Ice Hockey Team, Cammi led her teammates to a gold-medal finish at the Nagano Winter Olympic Games. She competed in all six games, with a point total of four goals and four assists. She was selected by her fellow American Olympians as U.S. flag bearer during the closing ceremony. Cammi is the all-time leading U.S. scorer at the World Championships with fifty-nine points (thirty-six goals and twenty-three assists).

Christian Athletes in Hockey

John Vanbiesbrouck

Pronunciation: van-BEES-brook
Birth date: September 4, 1963
Birthplace: Detroit, Michigan
Country: United States
Residence: Boca Raton, FL
Height: 5'8" (173 cm)
Weight: 175 lbs. (79 kg)

John Vanbiesbrouck has maintained his Christian testimony through personal tragedy, difficulties, and disappointments. In 1993 John's brother committed suicide. That same year he experienced more change when he was traded to the NHL Florida Panthers, a new team not expected to perform well. He and his wife Rosalinde faced another challenge when they learned their oldest son needed special schooling.

Speaking of those life experiences, John says, "For a professional athlete, it's easy to think you're better than anyone else. . . . You're in a dangerous place if you're looking at or trusting in yourself. You become like a dog chasing its tail."

John soon began attending the Panthers' chapel services, in search of answers to his many questions. While meeting with the team's chaplain, he placed his faith in Christ. Now he realizes that his trust in the Lord is the only thing that will sustain him in times of trouble.

John was selected by the New York Rangers in the fourth round of the NHL entry draft on June 10, 1981. The Florida Panthers took him in the NHL expansion draft on June 24, 1993. He signed as a free agent to the Philadelphia Flyers in 1998 and was traded to the New York Islanders in 2000. Most recently he has been with the New Jersey Devils, where he has excelled in the Stanley Cup playoffs.

John was also named to *The Sporting News* All-Star team (1985–86 and 1993–94) and the NHL All-Star team (1985–86). He played in the NHL All-Star Game (1994, 1996, and 1997) as well, but many think his greatest moments were as the goaltender for the U.S. Men's Ice Hockey Team at the 1998 Winter Olympic Games in Nagano.

Krissy Wendell

Birth date: September 12, 1981
Birthplace: Minneapolis, Minnesota
Country: United States
Residence: Brooklyn Park, Minnesota
Height: 5'7" (170 cm)
Weight: 155 lbs. (70 kg)

Some have called Krissy Wendell the best female hockey player in the United States. She scored 166 points (110 goals and 56 assists) for her high school team, taking them to a Minnesota State Championship. The next closest scorer had only forty goals.

Krissy has played on the Women's National Team twice (1998 and 1999) and is presently training with Team USA for the Salt Lake City Olympics.

But that's all just fun. The important stuff for Krissy is her relationship with God. "Making sure my relationship with God comes first," she says, is numero uno on her list of things to do in life. "When you're running a busy schedule, it's easy to put God on the back burner, to say, 'I'll pray tomorrow.' But when you put God first, things go so much better and your life is so much more at peace."

This is paramount in Krissy's mind as she pursues the opportunity to play hockey for the U.S. Olympic Team. "You've got to make sure that he's first and put in the time to actually build your relationship with Christ," she says. "Spend time reading the Bible, spend time with him in prayer. That's how you learn the most. It's how you can know that God is working in you and through you. That's what gives you peace."

Krissy grew up in a Christian home dedicated to the Lord. She accepted Christ as a young girl and then committed her life to him once again at a Fellowship of Christian Athletes (FCA) Sports Camp. She hopes that her life and career will influence young athletes in the same way hockey players impacted her when she was a young up-and-comer.

She's humble and a gifted player, eager to give her time to kids at camps and conferences. Kids see a person can be both a top player and a committed Christian. Her former coach, Bill Butters, sees Krissy as a real leader for the next generation.

Krissy is not the first hockey player in her family. Her father played hockey when he was young, and her older brother, who played for the University of Minnesota, was drafted by the Washington Capitals in 1998.

Krissy faced a difficult decision in 2000. She had to choose between college and training for the U.S. Olympic Team. "I really struggled with whether or not I should go to college or go out and train with the U.S. Team," she says. "Ultimately, my parents said, 'You need to keep praying about it and figure out what God wants you to do. When you decide, you'll know it's right, because you'll have a peace about it.'"

How did she resolve the struggle?

One of Krissy's favorite Bible verses is Psalm 37:4: "Delight yourself in the LORD and he will give you the desires of your heart."

"This verse gives me focus and reminds me that I don't have to worry about what's ahead of me. I can trust God and know that he will take me in the right path. There's no time limit on prayer. If you pray long enough, you'll know where God is leading you."

Krissy decided to stick with Team USA and has been traveling with them for the last two years, training and preparing for the ultimate challenge—the 2002 Winter Olympic Games.

She has always played for fun, saying she could play hockey all day, every day. But now she isn't in it just for fun. "I want a gold medal!" she says. "I want to be on the 2002 Team, and I want to win the gold."

Having the support of her family, her team, and her Lord, Krissy has all she needs to go all the way. We'll certainly be rooting for her and the team.

A Quick Look at Curling

Not many Americans are curling fans, but it is an old and much-followed sport in many parts of the world today. It began in sixteenth-century Scotland, where fellow Scots "curled" on frozen ponds, lochs, and marshes. Curling stones exist that date back to 1511. Evidence of sporting competitions can be documented all the way back to Paisley Abbey, Scotland, in 1541.

Early curlers took their stones from a riverbed, hurled them out along the ice at a certain target, and then used brooms to get the stones as close as possible. In the 1600s, handles were affixed to the stones, giving competitors a throw much like that seen in today's curling matches.

British troops brought curling to the United States in the 1850s.

Curling has only recently been added to the Olympic program, debuting at the 1998 Nagano Winter Games with both men's and women's competitions.

Canada won the women's gold medal in the last Olympics, besting Denmark 9–5 in the final. Switzerland defeated Canada 9–3, clinching the men's gold.

Curling:
> *Men*
> *Women*

8

LUGE

Archaeologists have found sleds that date back as far as A.D. 800. Vikings used sleds with two runners, much like today's version. The first international sled race was held in 1883 in Davos, Switzerland. Twenty-one competitors from Australia, England, Germany, the Netherlands, Sweden, Switzerland, and the United States did their best to finish first in a four-kilometer road race from St. Wolfgang to Klosters. Georg Robertson, a student from Australia, and Peter Minsch, a mailman from Klosters, won, finishing the race in just over nine minutes.

The luge made its Olympic debut at the 1964 Olympic Winter Games. Three events were held—men's, women's, and doubles. After the 1992 Winter Olympics, the doubles, which had always been men's doubles, was changed to mixed-gender doubles, although no mixed-gender teams have yet competed.

Photo by: Jamie Squire / Allsport

Since 1964, eighty-eight of ninety medals have been awarded to athletes from Germany, Austria, Italy, or the former Soviet Union. The United States has medaled only twice, taking the silver and bronze medals in the doubles competition at the 1998 Winter Olympic Games in Nagano.

Luge (sledding)
>*Men's singles*
>*Mixed-gender doubles*
>*Women's singles*

Olympic Watch

Clay Ives ▭▬▭▬▭▬▭

Birth date: September 5, 1972
Birthplace: Bancroft, Canada
Country: United States
Residence: Bancroft, Canada and Lake Placid, New York
Height: 5'10" (178 cm)
Weight: 165 lbs. (75 kg)

In earlier Olympic Games, Clay competed for the Canadians. Then in 1998, unhappy with the lack of financial support provided for luge by the Canadian government, Clay joined the U.S. Olympic Team. He was able to declare dual citizenship based on his family ties. Ranked fifteenth in the 1999–2000 World Cup standings, Clay races singles for the United States.

Brian Martin

Birth date: January 19, 1974
Birthplace: Stanford, California
Country: United States
Residence: Palo Alto, California
Height: 5'8" (173 cm)
Weight: 163 lbs. (74 kg)

Brian Martin made Olympic luge history for the United States at the 1998 Nagano Games. One U.S. team took the silver medal and Brian, along with his partner Mark Gimmette, walked away with the bronze. In the thirty-four-year Olympic history of the event, no American had ever won a medal.

Mark was the front driver and Brian the back driver when the two partnered in the summer of 1996. Without funding, they paid their own way to the World Cup competition in Lillehammer, Norway. After taking the bronze medal, the U.S. Luge Federation stepped in to back them. Brian and Mark won four out of six World Cup events during the 1997–98 season, taking the overall title. They have also won the bronze medals at the last two World Championships (1999, 2000).

A Christian Athlete in Luge

Anne Abernathy

Birth date: April 12, 1953
Birthplace: Eglin Air Force Base, Florida

Country: U. S. Virgin Islands
Residence: Calgary, Canada
Height: 5'5" (165 cm)
Weight: 160 lbs. (72 kg)

Anne Abernathy is one of only four or five women to have competed in four Winter Olympic Games. In Nagano, she was the oldest woman ever to compete. Anne comes from St. Thomas, one of the U. S. Virgin Islands.

Anne's age has always been a novelty. When she made her first Olympic appearance in 1988 at the age of 35, Anne was the oldest person competing in her sport—and that has been true ever since. In 1994 at the Lillehammer Games, a fellow contestant nicknamed her "Grandma Luge."

Anne went to high school and trains in Virginia, but she lives in the Virgin Islands and competes for them.

Anne knows a great deal about the kind of perseverance an Olympic athlete must develop in order to compete successfully. Since 1988, she has suffered from lymphatic cancer, but she has not allowed it to knock her out of competition. Until an article unveiled her disease a few years ago, most people on the circuit had no idea that she was ill. Anne has also crashed several times in competition, resulting in broken bones and injuries to her knees and shoulder that required surgery.

Anne planned to compete in five World Cup races before Christmas of 2001 in preparation for the 2002 Winter Olympic Games. But she was fighting several illnesses that could crush her hopes of making a fifth appearance at the Winter Olympic Games.

Anne went to church as a young person, but she did not become a Christian until she entered college. During the first couple of weeks at Salisbury University in Salisbury, Maryland, she attended an orientation party. A young man who had had too much to drink and was not a student asked her to dance. To avoid an awkward situation, she walked over to a man who was wearing a cross and asked him to dance with her. Later, the man asked her why she had chosen him.

Anne said, "I mentioned his cross, and he asked if I was a Christian. I said no, it hadn't been proven to me. I'd gone to church my whole life but wasn't a believer. He made a bet with me that by the next morning, I'd be a Christian. We bet lunch. He lost that bet, but at lunch he began answering all my questions. When I'd ask a question, he'd stop to pray and then give me an answer. By the next morning at breakfast, he had shared the whole story of the Bible with me. I was sitting in the middle of the student union, and I accepted Christ on the spot. It was pretty wild."

One of the most difficult things for Christians in sports is to find fellowship on the road. Anne has a support group at home made up of single women—divorcees, single parents, and widows. Though they don't always understand what she does, Anne is grateful for their prayers and support.

Her strongest support group, though, is in Calgary, Canada. She says, "There I have a Bible study with a group of athletes that I consider my support group. I am very close to them."

How has her faith helped her in luge, a sport in which you sled at speeds up to eighty miles an hour down a track you can't really see? She says, "My faith has helped me so much. Until the last two Olympics, I'd been kind of a solitary Christian. Then I started going to church, and it made all the difference. It's extremely difficult to medal in my sport, particularly if you're not from Germany. Germany has won the last thirty-five World Cup races. It's also a struggle when you're in the sport and you're not funded. I spend ninety percent of my time just explaining to people what the sport of luge is. There's no instant identification with the sport like hurdles or swimming."

That kind of struggle is what the Olympics, sports, and life is all about. "It's not the gold, but the goal," she often says.

Anne has had nine surgeries on her knees, and has gone through chemotherapy and radiation therapy. It's a struggle to keep coming back to the Olympics. But she has felt God's presence in amazing ways. "One of the things in my sport that is necessary is to be able to go full out lying on your back, feet first, not being able to really look at the track. At the 1994 Olympic Games, I really felt the Lord was with me. I had such confidence. On the first run, though, I didn't look [down the track]. That was incredible. I had a little ping-ponging on that run (when you hit the sides of the course). But I felt so good.

"Then on the next run, I remember sitting up and looking out at the sky. It was so cold, the water molecules were freezing and the air was sparkling. I was thinking, *Man, I'm here.* So I said a prayer. 'Lord, you got me here. Why don't you come along for the ride?' And on that whole run down, I felt like there was an angel hanging on the back of my sled, going with me on the run. That whole competition gave me such peace, even though I didn't win. It made me realize there's a lot more to competition than winning a medal."

Later a reporter asked her if she had had any unusual experience during the Games. "Yes, but you'll never print it," she said. That comment only made the reporter more determined. "So I told her the angel story," Anne says, "And the story came out on the front page of the newspaper. It said, 'She prayed at the start and an angel flew with her down the track.' That blew me away!"

Perseverance is a big issue with Anne. Just getting to the Olympics the first time was one of the greatest struggles of her life.

Before the 1988 Olympics, Anne had two setbacks. In 1986, she battled lymphatic carcinoma, a kind of cancer. Then in 1987, she crashed at Lake Placid and had a double fracture of her knee. At that point, she was asking herself why she even wanted to go to the Olympics. She wasn't sure, but she knew she wanted to do it. She trained, got into shape, and made it to the 1988 Winter Olympic Games, where she competed well despite the setbacks.

One of Anne's greatest moments occurred when she walking into the opening ceremonies in 1988. Anne says, "When you've worked for years to get to the Olympic Games, it's unbelievable to walk into that arena with all the different countries and people. Leading up to that Olympics, no one knew I had cancer. My parents didn't know. My Olympic committee didn't know. I didn't tell anyone because I was afraid they wouldn't let me go.

"The week before the competition, once I had been entered and been accredited, I told my parents and the committee. I didn't want it to leak out and them to be surprised or anything.

"Then after my final run, I was ecstatic that I'd been able to compete, the first person ever to compete for the Virgin Islands in the Winter Olympics. I finished sixteenth.

"I don't think winning a medal would have been as emotional as just getting there. One doctor had told me I'd never make it. So it was a great moment."

What does Anne tell young people who ask about her sport?

"I really don't think you should always focus on getting a gold medal," she says, "In the U.S., all the advertising is about going for the gold. I hate that because it really should be, 'Go for the goal.' Your victory is not necessarily getting a gold medal; it could be just getting there and performing."

She links this to her faith and understanding of the Bible.

"If you go back to the original Olympic Games and even in the Bible when Paul talks about the Games," she says, "competing for the prize, what they're competing for was a crown, a laurel wreath. Not even a gold medal. It's not being number one that's important. That's not where the victory comes."

Anne has many favorite Bible verses. One of her favorites is the parable of the widow in Luke 18:1–8. The widow keeps knocking on the judge's door, asking him for justice. Anne sees herself as being much like that widow—coming back again and again to ask God for help.

Another passage she loves is Luke 11:5–13, which admonishes Christians to be bold when they ask God for something. She says, "A lot of verses about hardship are the ones I think about. Hebrews 12:1–12, that whole passage about perseverance and discipline. It talks about how you need to persevere and how it hurts and how you have to be disciplined. I think of that every time I'm on a treadmill. 'Strengthen your feeble arms and weak knees.' I think the Lord wrote that just for me.

"I also like the one in 1 Corinthians 9:24–27 about running your race, that you should run in such a way to get the prize. And we run to get a crown that will last forever. We buffet our bodies so we won't be disqualified."

She adds, "There are so many verses that talk about competing. Second Timothy 2:5 about the athlete who must compete according to the rules or he won't receive the prize. I think that relates to sportsmanship as well. I think it's more important to compete for Christ and please Christ than to win the gold and be so conceited afterwards that people just go, 'Yicccchhh!' If your life changes after you win a gold medal, I have to ask, is that a good thing?"

One of the things that has most influenced her is a quote from de Coubertin, who founded the Olympic Games in 1896. "He has a quote that says, 'The most important thing in life is not the triumph, but the struggle. The essential thing is not to have conquered, but to have fought well,'" Anne says. "I look at that, and I think I want to get to the Olympics and I want to win a medal, but the struggle is what has really taught me and made me grow. Getting to the Games isn't the whole thing. When I crashed in 1994, I knew I had still done my best. So that reminds me of that truth."

Anne says she has been greatly influenced by the competitors from Germany. "The German women also have been helpful to me," she says. "I haven't had my own coach, but the German women have been there in a way a coach would. From helping me carry my equipment to telling me how to take a run, they've been great. I have trained with them. Three or four of them have befriended me, and they're all champions. Everyone on the German team is a champion at some level. Yet they take the time to help someone like me who is about as far away from the podium as you can get. They can be winners and haven't lost touch. That impresses me."

Anne has had a long and eventful history of Olympic competition. If you see her in Salt Lake, tell her, "It's not the gold but the goal," and you will make her smile.

9

BOBSLEIGH

For many years, it was universally believed that bobsleigh began in Switzerland in the late 1800s. However, before the Nagano Games in 1998, it was discovered that lumber sleds were raced in Albany, New York, in the 1880s. Regardless of which came first, bobsleigh is an old and revered sport, which debuted at the 1924 Olympic Winter Games in Chamonix, France.

At the 1924 Winter Games, bobsleigh was a five-man event. But by the 1928 Olympics, it had become a four-man competition. Two-man bobsleigh was added at the 1932 Lake Placid Games. The first women's bobsleigh competition will take place at the 2002 Winter Olympics.

In the bobsleigh competitions, two-person or four-person sleds race down an inclined track at least 1,500 meters long. The track includes fifteen to twenty turns of up to 180 degrees each. Racers often reach speeds of more than one hundred miles per hour.

Photo by: Matthew Stockman / Allsport

Bobsleigh (two types of sleds down a course):
    Four-Man Bobsleigh
    Two-Man Bobsleigh
    Four-Woman Bobsleigh
    Two-Woman Bobsleigh

Olympic Watch

Bonny Warner

Birth date: April 7, 1962
Birthplace: Mt. Baldy, California
Country: United States
Residence: Discovery Bay, California
Height: 5'8" (173 cm)
Weight: 150 lbs. (68 kg)

Bonny has run the luge in three previous Olympic Games (1984, 1988, and 1992) and will make her bobsleigh debut in Salt Lake City. Retired from luge in 1992, Bonny decided to participate in bobsleigh after it was included in the 2002 Olympic program. She placed fifth at the 2000 World Championships and ninth in 2001. She captured silver medals in the last two World Cup races.

A Christian Athlete in Bobsleigh

Sheridon Baptiste (Canada)

Birth date: June 1, 1964
Birthplace: Georgetown, Guyana, S.A.
Country: Canada
Residence: Ottawa, Ontario
Height: 6'0" (185 cm)
Weight: 193 lbs. (86 kg)

After several years trying to break into Canadian football, Sheridon Baptiste received an invitation to try out for the Canadian Olympic Bobsleigh Team. He made it as the bobsleigh brakeman, and the rest is history. Sheridon has competed in one Olympics (1994—Lillehammer), where his team finished eleventh, and in several World Championships, placing in the top ten four times in the four-man and two times in the two-man bobsleigh competition.

Sheridon and his family came to Canada from Guyana, South America, in 1976. It had been a difficult time for the Baptiste family. Sheridon's parents were considering divorce when his mother decided to relocate to Canada, where she had grown up.

When did Sheridon's faith journey begin?

"I don't have a long story," he says. "I grew up in a Christian family. My first conscious decision about Christ came when I was about seventeen. I was trying to determine whether to attend a Christian school. It was a tough decision because the school didn't have interscholastic sports. I did a lot of praying, and in the end, I decided to go. When I made the decision, the Spirit really came over me, and I felt strongly I had done the right thing. Even today I remember it as a really beautiful feeling.

"As I attended the school, I knew I really needed to be there. I didn't miss sports that much—which was odd. I joined the choir. Being there brought me close to God. It was a great time."

While attending Christian school, Sheridon was away from sports for about a year and a half. But he feels it was probably the best time of spiritual growth he can remember. After high school, Sheridon attended Queens University, where he was heavily involved in track and field, basketball, and football.

How does Sheridon's faith impact his sport?

"With Christ I know that nothing can be taken away from me," he says. "I believe you have to work hard and do your best. But it doesn't matter how much we do and accumulate, because we can't do it without Christ. That's always in the back of my mind. Many people say that when you find Christ you're going to lose a lot of your edge and your desire to compete. For me, it's the opposite. It [my faith in Christ] makes me persevere and carry on."

How does Sheridon show his faith as he competes in sporting events?

With a laugh, he says, "I was trying out with the Ottawa Rough Riders in 1994, a football team in the CFL. One day at practice, this guy came out of nowhere and leveled me. The play was over, the whistle had blown, but he whaled me, knocked me right on my face. Obviously, I was upset. He stood over me like he was ready to fight or something. My first instinct was that he had just wronged me, and I should do something about it—retaliate. I was about to get up. But a smile came on my face. I lifted my hand and said, 'Nice hit.' Shock registered on his face; he was ready to fight. From that time on, though, we helped each other out."

What were some of Sheridon's greatest moments?

"Back in 1995, right after the Lillehammer Olympics," he says, "I competed in Canada in track and field. I was on a relay team that won the gold in special games held in Paris. I was the only unproven member of the team, and there was a lot of pressure on me. But we pulled it out and won. I ran the first leg.

"It was almost a feeling as if it wasn't me running. I don't remember hardly anything except just running all out. It's kind of hard to describe, because you're thinking about not letting your teammates down. But it was like God was with me, and I just ran fantastically."

One other event stands out in Sheridon's memory—the day he finally beat his sister in a footrace! "I was nine or ten. She was always the fastest. She was my big sister. And I beat her. It was in our village in Guyana. We'd see who was the fastest to get to the village. But I got her. That was some moment."

Sheridon's favorite Bible verse is Philippians 2:3–5: "Do nothing out of selfish ambition or vain conceit, but in humility consider others better than yourselves. Each of you should look not only to your own interests, but also to the interests of others."

"You see so many athletes today where everything is rah-rah—they're in your face. The humility

thing really hits me. I look at television and there
aren't that many athletes who have that spirit of
humility. That bothers me a bit. God uses all of us.
It doesn't matter who we are or how we personally
think about what we're doing and saying. God will
work through us to get his work done."

Who are the heroes in Sheridon's life?

"My mother has influenced me greatly," he says.
"She raised four kids on a nurse's salary. She put all
four of us through college. My church has done a lot,
but my mom has always led by example through her
words, her work, and the way she treats others.

"My newest hero is my wife. She's very spiritual, but she also started a software company and
has made it go."

What would he say to young people today who
might dream of competing in the Olympic Games?

"One of my principles in life," he says, "is that
we should always give more than people expect and
always do it cheerfully. That has helped me in
sports. A lot of sport is about failing. We all fail. But
we should do our sport with a cheerful attitude, go
beyond what people expect.

"Life is also about choices. I say that you should
always make the choices that honor God."

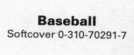

We want to hear from you. Please send your comments about this book to us in care of the address below. Thank you.

Zonder**kidz**™

Grand Rapids, MI 49530
www.zonderkidz.com